Companion to the Sunday Gospels

Year B

by
Henry Wansbrough, OSB

All booklets are published thanks to the generous support of the members of the Catholic Truth Society

CATHOLIC TRUTH SOCIETY
PUBLISHERS TO THE HOLY SEE

ISBN 978 1 78469 194 3

Introduction

This year the Sunday Gospel readings are taken from Mark, except for those of several Sundays before and after Easter, which come from John. Mark is almost certainly the earliest gospel-writer, putting together in his own words the stories which were being told about Jesus. The prominence of Peter in the Gospel suggests that many of them may have come from Peter, but other people would also have handed on their experiences of Jesus. Mark speaks with an easy, direct style, and is a superb story-teller; that may be why the community asked him to tell the story of Jesus. He stresses that it is not always easy to understand Jesus, and that his disciples must also take up the cross of Jesus to follow him.

A good way to use this book is to set aside a regular time, either alone or with others. Try to find a quiet space in your life. Aware that the word of the Lord brings us life and carries us into the Lord's own company, read the gospel-passage once or twice slowly and reflectively. Then read the meditation on the passage. Give it all time to sink in, and stop to pray whenever you feel moved to do so. It may help to share your thoughts with others and in turn to listen to their reflections. Finally read the gospel again. Always end with a prayer and try to put into words one message that you have received from the reading.

Jesus said to his disciples: 'Be on your guard, stay awake, because you never know when the time will come. It is like a man travelling abroad: he has gone from home, and left his servants in charge, each with his own task; and he has told the doorkeeper to stay awake. So stay awake, because you do not know when the master of the house is coming, evening, midnight, cockcrow, dawn; if he comes unexpectedly, he must not find you asleep. And what I say to you I say to all: Stay awake!'

The Watcher at the Door

This brief parable of the master returning unexpectedly is typical of Jesus's vivid way of speaking. The message is typical, too, for Jesus was constantly stressing that there is no time to lose. In the Gospel of Mark especially there is a feeling of hurry: in chapter one alone there are fourteen instances of 'immediately'! When Jesus came in his earthly ministry he again and again challenged his hearers to make up their minds NOW, to change their ways NOW. He challenges us to do the same. We can hear the rattle of the returning Master's key in the lock. There is no time to hide the contraband, to pull our uniforms straight before greeting the Master at his entry. Even if we do not think that the world's end is imminent, even if death is not threatening, every moment counts, every decision is for or against Jesus. Saints are rumoured to have said that, if they were to receive the news that they were to die that night, they would carry on doing what they were doing anyway.

Is this really a Christian attitude? If we need to put things a bit more in order to prepare for the Lord's coming, is there any valid reason to delay? The four weeks of Advent are anyway a good time to clean things up for the Lord's coming.

Question: What do I need to change in my lifestyle?

The beginning of the Good News about Jesus Christ, the Son of God. It is written in the book of the prophet Isaiah:

> Look, I am going to send my messenger
>   before you;
> he will prepare your way.
> A voice cries in the wilderness:
> Prepare a way for the Lord,
>   make his paths straight,

and so it was that John the Baptist appeared in the wilderness, proclaiming a baptism of repentance for the forgiveness of sins. All Judaea and all the people of Jerusalem made their way to him, and as they were baptised by him in the river Jordan they confessed their sins. John wore a garment of camel-skin, and he lived on locusts and wild honey. In the course of his preaching he said, 'Someone is following me, someone who is more powerful than I am, and I am not fit to kneel down and undo the strap of his sandals. I have baptised you with water, but he will baptise you with the Holy Spirit.'

A Baptism for Conversion

Each Advent has two John-the-Baptist Sundays, the first when we see John preparing a community for the Messiah, the second when he points out Jesus as the Lamb of God. Today is the first of these. John chose a point where the busy road from Jerusalem to the East crossed the Jordan River. There he button-holed all the busy financiers, merchants and other travellers and tourists, warning them to change their ways – and to change them now, before it was too late. 'I am too busy,' no doubt they said, 'I have other things to worry about; I have a wife and family to feed.' John was forming a community of repentance, but not so much a community which wept 'Boo-hoo!' about their sins, as a community of people determined to set their scale of values right. He meant them to stop going in one direction, to turn around and go in a different direction. Do we give ourselves a moment of pause to ask whether we have our priorities right? Where on our list of priorities does the entry of Christ into our lives come? John said rotten trees were going to be cut down, useless straw to be burnt. Do I need to feel the axe at my feet?

Question: What would happen if I turned my life around?

A man came, sent by God.
His name was John.
He came as a witness,
as a witness to speak for the light,
so that everyone might believe through him.
He was not the light,
only a witness to speak for the light.

This is how John appeared as a witness. When the Jews sent priests and Levites from Jerusalem to ask him, 'Who are you?' he not only declared, but he declared quite openly, 'I am not the Christ.' 'Well then,' they asked 'are you Elijah?' 'I am not' he said. 'Are you the Prophet?' He answered, 'No.' So they said to him, 'Who are you? We must take back an answer to those who sent us. What have you to say about yourself?' So John said, 'I am, as Isaiah prophesied:

a voice that cries in the wilderness:
Make a straight way for the Lord.'

Now these men had been sent by the Pharisees, and they put this further question to him, 'Why are you baptising if you are not the Christ, and not Elijah, and not the prophet?' John replied, 'I baptise with water, but there stands among you – unknown to you – the one who is coming after me; and I am not fit to undo his sandal-strap.' This happened at Bethany, on the far side of the Jordan, where John was baptising.

A Voice Crying in the Desert

So, John the Baptist came as a witness to the light. In today's gospel reading he seems rather to refuse witness. He is quite negative, answering with a stalwart and repeated 'No!' He witnesses only 'There is one standing among you whom you do not know'. It is not always easy to find Jesus. All the way through the Gospel of John there are misunderstandings about Jesus, as people fail to recognise him for what he is: the Samaritan at the well, Nicodemus, Mary Magdalene beside the empty tomb, even Peter and the disciples as they fish on the lake. We can easily become so wrapped up in our own troubles and worries that we fail to recognise the one figure who can bring their solution, although he is standing among us, the one who 'has the words of eternal life'. He may come to us in a way we do not like, as a corrective, blocking or diverting the way we had chosen. He may come as suffering, disappointment, failure or bereavement. All of these may be acts of God's love, to show us the way, though we cannot see it at the time. It is just like John the Baptist, saying steadily 'No!', until eventually we turn around and see Christ as our true light.

Question: Does Christ confront us in a John-the-Baptist way? How?

The angel Gabriel was sent by God to a town in Galilee called Nazareth, to a virgin betrothed to a man named Joseph, of the house of David; and the virgin's name was Mary. He went in and said to her, 'Rejoice, so highly favoured! The Lord is with you.' She was deeply disturbed by these words and asked herself what this greeting could mean, but the angel said to her, 'Mary, do not be afraid; you have won God's favour. Listen! You are to conceive and bear a son, and you must name him Jesus. He will be great and will be called Son of the Most High. The Lord God will give him the throne of his ancestor David; he will rule over the House of Jacob for ever and his reign will have no end.' Mary said to the angel, 'But how can this come about, since I am a virgin?' 'The Holy Spirit will come upon you', the angel answered, 'and the power of the Most High will cover you with its shadow. And so the child will be holy and will be called Son of God. Know this too: your kinswoman Elizabeth has, in her old age, conceived a son, and she whom people called barren is now in her sixth month, for nothing is impossible to God.' 'I am the handmaid of the Lord,' said Mary, 'let what you have said be done to me.' And the angel left her.

The Annunciation

As we prepare for the birth of Jesus, the final Sunday of Advent always focuses on Mary. What was the young girl Mary doing when the message came? Kneeling piously? Feeding the sheep? Fetching water? Sweeping the mud floor? What was she thinking? Engaged to be married, surely about her approaching wedding to Joseph and about the children she would mother? Then came the message which she could accept or refuse, the message on which hung the future of the world: her child would be different from all others. How 'different'? Her thoughts were turned back to the promise to David. It had been read to her so often in the Bible, and now the words were drummed into her mind: 'his reign will have no end'. This would all be the work of the Spirit which she had so often heard read out in Isaiah; 'the Holy Spirit will come upon you', the Spirit which was to come upon the Servant of the Lord, the Spirit of Emmanuel, 'God with us'. Her young body was to grow, nourish and develop this child. Then she would have the child in her arms to cherish and shape as both Son of God and her own son.

Question: How is the Immaculate Conception related to Mary's motherhood?

When the day came for them to be purified as laid down by the Law of Moses, the parents of Jesus took him up to Jerusalem to present him to the Lord – observing what stands written in the Law of the Lord: 'Every first-born male must be consecrated to the Lord' – and also to offer in sacrifice, in accordance with what is said in the Law of the Lord, 'a pair of turtledoves or two young pigeons'. Now in Jerusalem there was a man named Simeon. He was an upright and devout man; he looked forward to Israel's comforting and the Holy Spirit rested on him. It had been revealed to him by the Holy Spirit that he would not see death until he had set eyes on the Christ of the Lord. Prompted by the Spirit he came to the Temple; and when the parents brought in the child Jesus to do for him what the Law required, he took him into his arms and blessed God; and he said:

'Now, Master, you can let your servant
    go in peace,
just as you promised;
because my eyes have seen the salvation
which you have prepared for all the nations
    to see,
a light to enlighten the gentiles
and the glory of your people Israel.'

As the child's father and mother stood there wondering at the things that were being said about him, Simeon blessed them and said to Mary his mother, 'You see this child: he is destined for the fall and for the rising of many in Israel, destined to be a sign that is rejected – and a sword will pierce your own soul too – so that the secret thoughts of many may be laid bare.'

There was a prophetess also, Anna the daughter of Phanuel, of the tribe of Asher. She was well on in years. Her days of girlhood over, she had been married for seven years before becoming a widow. She was now eighty-four years old and never left the Temple, serving God night and day with fasting and prayer. She came by just at that moment and began to praise God; and she spoke of the child to all who looked forward to the deliverance of Jerusalem.

When they had done everything the Law of the Lord required, they went back to Galilee, to their own town of Nazareth. Meanwhile the child grew to maturity, and he was filled with wisdom; and God's favour was with him.

The Presentation in the Temple

The story of the Presentation of the child Jesus in the Temple is dominated by Simeon's welcome, 'a light to enlighten the gentiles and the glory of your people Israel', and by his warning to Mary, 'a sword will pierce your heart'. Simeon reiterates the angel's promise that the child would fulfil the destiny of Israel and Israel's task to the nations. Much as in any family life, the promised future included the delights of the growing, developing child, and the background fear that the great destiny of each child may include sorrow and even heartbreak. How much did Mary and Joseph know about the precious child they were nurturing? As he grew to independence did he become more loving and supportive? How did his contemporaries find him? Was he a leader? Did he stand out from the pack? Each of us has a private picture of the child, the boy, the adolescent, the young man. All we know for sure is that 'the child grew to maturity', and that Mary 'pondered all these things in her heart', with Simeon's welcome and warning before her mind.

Question: What would Mary have felt and thought as she went home from the Temple?

MATTHEW 2:1-12

After Jesus had been born at Bethlehem in Judaea during the reign of King Herod, some wise men came to Jerusalem from the east. 'Where is the infant king of the Jews?' they asked. 'We saw his star as it rose and have come to do him homage.' When King Herod heard this he was perturbed, and so was the whole of Jerusalem. He called together all the chief priests and the scribes of the people, and enquired of them where the Christ was to be born. 'At Bethlehem in Judaea,' they told him 'for this is what the prophet wrote:

> And you, Bethlehem, in the land of Judah,
> you are by no means least among the leaders of Judah,
> for out of you will come a leader
> who will shepherd my people Israel.'

Then Herod summoned the wise men to see him privately. He asked them the exact date on which the star had appeared, and sent them on to Bethlehem. 'Go and find out all about the child,' he said 'and when you have found him, let me know, so that I too may go and do him homage.' Having listened to what the king had to say, they set out. And there in front of them was the star they had seen rising; it went forward and halted over the place where the child was. The sight of the star filled them with delight, and going into the house they saw the child with his mother Mary, and falling to their knees they did him homage. Then, opening their treasures, they offered him gifts of gold and frankincense and myrrh. But they were warned in a dream not to go back to Herod, and returned to their own country by a different way.

Wise Men from the East

The Wise Men, with their clever knowledge of astronomy and their lavish gifts, represent all that is best in worldly values. They also have a bit of magic about them, for frankincense and myrrh were used in spells, and the word for 'wise men' can also mean 'magicians'. They have real wisdom and its reward, and yet they lay it all at Jesus's feet. It might be worth asking at this beginning of the year whether we submit all our skills and comforts to Jesus. It is not humility – just a true scale of values.

The story also rests on the sharp contrast between King Herod and the Wise Men. Herod was a Jew, so he should have recognised and honoured the Jewish Messiah. Not at all! He tries to kill the Messiah. By contrast, the Wise Men, arriving from the equivalent of Outer Space, carry on their search till they find Jesus and humbly bow before him. This poses a nasty question: we Christians have all the guidance and encouragement of the Church, but how often we find those outside the Church, not even professed Christians, behaving in a more Christian way than we do ourselves!

Question: What skill can I submit to Jesus today?

As John stood with two of his disciples, Jesus passed, and John stared hard at him and said, 'Look, there is the lamb of God.' Hearing this, the two disciples followed Jesus. Jesus turned round, saw them following and said, 'What do you want?' They answered, 'Rabbi,' – which means Teacher – 'where do you live?' 'Come and see' he replied; so they went and saw where he lived, and stayed with him the rest of that day. It was about the tenth hour.

One of these two who became followers of Jesus after hearing what John had said was Andrew, the brother of Simon Peter. Early next morning, Andrew met his brother and said to him 'We have found the Messiah' – which means the Christ – and he took Simon to Jesus. Jesus looked hard at him and said, 'You are Simon son of John; you are to be called Cephas' – meaning Rock.

The First Disciples

This year the ordinary Sunday gospel readings are taken from Mark, enabling us to get a full picture of that Gospel. But Mark is the shortest of the gospels, and is not quite long enough, so just occasionally a reading from John slips in to complete the picture.

This story of the call of the first disciples takes place in the Jordan Valley, where John was baptising. The first two to be called are disciples of John, so had joined his group of those waiting for the Messiah. They were ready when John pointed him out. It is striking that Jesus first calls them to be with him, and first of all they remain with him for a time. First in our call to follow Christ comes prayer and getting to know Christ, before we can actively work for Christ and bring others to share his joy. Only after this repose with Jesus do they sprint off in their enthusiasm and bring others to join in the benefits they have received from the tranquillity of keeping company with Jesus.

Question: As a disciple of Jesus, do I spend enough time simply being with him?

After John had been arrested, Jesus went into Galilee. There he proclaimed the Good News from God. 'The time has come' he said 'and the kingdom of God is close at hand. Repent, and believe the Good News.'

As he was walking along by the Sea of Galilee he saw Simon and his brother Andrew casting a net in the lake – for they were fishermen. And Jesus said to them, 'Follow me and I will make you into fishers of men.' And at once they left their nets and followed him.

Going on a little further, he saw James son of Zebedee and his brother John; they too were in their boat, mending their nets. He called them at once and, leaving their father Zebedee in the boat with the men he employed, they went after him.

The Call of the Disciples

What is going on? Last Sunday we had the story of the first two disciples joining Jesus. One of them was Andrew, the other unnamed. Now we get another story, in another place, of other first disciples being called. So the Church underlines, two weeks running, the importance of Jesus's new community. The first thing he does is call disciples. He can't do everything on his own, and that is the point of the Church. He calls disciples to make a new people, a new Israel. We all have our part to fill in Jesus's play (sometimes it seems like a pantomime), old, young, middle-aged. Tired old people, busy parents, lively youngsters, each of us can make a unique contribution, especially since Jesus has chosen us himself. An odd choice, some of us! What did he want ME to do in the new family of Jesus?

The two different places show that at least two different people told the story. When two people tell the same story, there are bound to be variations. The place didn't matter, or the order in which the disciples were called. The point of the story was the call, the response and the companionship, working together.

Question: Whom would you point to as having left everything to follow Jesus?

Jesus and his followers went as far as Capernaum, and as soon as the Sabbath came Jesus went to the synagogue and began to teach. And his teaching made a deep impression on them because, unlike the scribes, he taught them with authority.

In their synagogue just then there was a man possessed by an unclean spirit, and it shouted, 'What do you want with us, Jesus of Nazareth? Have you come to destroy us? I know who you are: the Holy One of God.' But Jesus said sharply, 'Be quiet! Come out of him!' And the unclean spirit threw the man into convulsions and with a loud cry went out of him. The people were so astonished that they started asking each other what it all meant. 'Here is a teaching that is new' they said 'and with authority behind it: he gives orders even to unclean spirits and they obey him.' And his reputation rapidly spread everywhere, through all the surrounding Galilean countryside.

Jesus Teaches with Authority

This story goes one step further in showing the growing authority of Jesus, which is the theme of the early part of Mark's Gospel. He has already called the disciples. He calls and they simply follow. It seems that he is a total stranger to them, yet with such authority that they drop everything to follow him. Now in the synagogue he teaches on his own authority. He does not quote the interpretations of others, as rabbinic teachers did, saying, 'Rabbi X says this, Rabbi Y says that'. No. Jesus teaches, 'I say to you...' He seems to be master even of the Law. But it is God's Law. Only God has authority over it, so who does he think he is? At least he is the teacher comparable to Moses, who is to come into the world, the teacher prophesied in today's first reading. Then, to confirm his authoritative teaching he shows his authority by overcoming the dreaded unclean spirit, wringing from it the snivelling protest, 'Have you come to destroy us?' and the acknowledgement that he has a special link with God.

Question: On the human level, why did people follow Jesus so enthusiastically?

On leaving the synagogue, Jesus went with James and John straight to the house of Simon and Andrew. Now Simon's mother-in-law had gone to bed with fever, and they told him about her straightaway. He went to her, took her by the hand and helped her up. And the fever left her and she began to wait on them.

That evening, after sunset, they brought to him all who were sick and those who were possessed by devils. The whole town came crowding round the door, and he cured many who were suffering from diseases of one kind or another; he also cast out many devils, but he would not allow them to speak, because they knew who he was.

In the morning, long before dawn, he got up and left the house, and went off to a lonely place and prayed there. Simon and his companions set out in search of him; and when they found him they said, 'Everybody is looking for you.' He answered, 'Let us go elsewhere, to the neighbouring country towns, so that I can preach there too, because that is why I came.' And he went all through Galilee, preaching in their synagogues and casting out devils.

Jesus at Capernaum

The snippets gathered in the gospel reading give us a sample of Jesus's activity at Capernaum, the little fishing village on the edge of the Lake of Galilee: healing and prayer. The first incident, the healing of the relative of his friend and follower Simon Peter, reminds us that Jesus does respond if we pray for the needs of our nearest and dearest. Then the summary of his evening activity shows his concern to bring healing and wholeness. Just so any Christian will desire to follow his example: we can harm or heal those around us in so many ways. It does not need to be a miracle! A greeting, a look, a smile, a touch can bring the peace of Christ to someone in desperate need of reassurance – and no less can they harm and wound. But the third little story, of Jesus going off to pray in the early morning, shows that the well-spring of all his activity was his union with the God whom he called his Father. We cannot say what Jesus's prayer was, any more than I can say what your prayer is, but the confident communication between Father and Son must have been the source of his strength and compassion.

Question: What is the best time and circumstance for prayer?

A leper came to Jesus and pleaded on his knees: 'If you want to' he said 'you can cure me.' Feeling sorry for him, Jesus stretched out his hand and touched him. 'Of course I want to!' he said. 'Be cured!' And the leprosy left him at once and he was cured. Jesus immediately sent him away and sternly ordered him, 'Mind you say nothing to anyone, but go and show yourself to the priest, and make the offering for your healing prescribed by Moses as evidence of your recovery.' The man went away, but then started talking about it freely and telling the story everywhere, so that Jesus could no longer go openly into any town, but had to stay outside in places where nobody lived. Even so, people from all around would come to him.

Jesus Heals a Leper

Mark shows the warmth of Jesus's humanity and his concern for the leper. The leper had no right even to approach Jesus, but must have felt that he would get a favourable response, no word of reproach. 'Jesus felt sorry for him' is a weak expression; the Greek is far stronger: colloquially it is literally translated 'was gutted'; Jesus felt it to the depths of his being. Then Jesus touched him, both touching someone ritually impure and risking the infection. There have been famous repetitions of this brave and heartfelt gesture: Francis of Assisi kissing a leper's hand, Princess Diana shaking hands with an AIDS sufferer (when the sickness was thought to be contagious by touch). One can imagine the awestruck horror of the bystanders at this outrageous expression of love and sympathy. Why, then, does Jesus 'sternly send him away'? A more faithful rendering would be not 'sternly' but 'in anger'. It is possible that the anger is directed at the leprosy, considered as an exterior invasion, so 'sent *it* away'. At least Jesus's whole-hearted emotional involvement with the sufferer is palpable.

Question: Why was Jesus so moved, or even angry, about the leprosy?

The Spirit drove Jesus out into the wilderness and he remained there for forty days, and was tempted by Satan. He was with the wild beasts, and the angels looked after him.

After John had been arrested, Jesus went into Galilee. There he proclaimed the Good News from God. 'The time has come' he said 'and the kingdom of God is close at hand. Repent, and believe the Good News.'

Jesus is Tested in the Desert

Each year the gospel reading for this Sunday is about Jesus's testing in the desert. Mark's emphasis is distinctly different from that of Matthew and Luke. No details of the testing, but rather Jesus's sojourn in the desert as almost a return to the peace of the Garden of Eden. The desert of Judaea, between Jerusalem and the Jordan Valley, is a noble and dignified solitude of smooth, sandstone hills. Nothing grows, of course, but wild camels and the occasional leopard prowl around. There Jesus was 'with the wild animals' as, led by the Spirit, he made his preparation for his mission. In what way was he tested? We may presume that in solitude and prayer he was working out the implications of the Voice from Heaven at his Baptism. How was he to run his course as the beloved Servant of the Lord? Precisely how was he to bring the presence of the Kingship of God into people's lives? The 'forty' is often used in biblical accounts for a period of preparation, as in Israel's forty years in the desert, or the apostles' forty days of preparation between Easter and Ascension. We may use our forty days to reflect on how we may bring God's presence to bear in and through our lives.

Question: Is testing the most important aspect of Lent?

Jesus took with him Peter and James and John and led them up a high mountain where they could be alone by themselves. There in their presence he was transfigured: his clothes became dazzlingly white, whiter than any earthly bleacher could make them. Elijah appeared to them with Moses; and they were talking with Jesus. Then Peter spoke to Jesus: 'Rabbi,' he said 'it is wonderful for us to be here; so let us make three tents, one for you, one for Moses and one for Elijah.' He did not know what to say; they were so frightened. And a cloud came, covering them in shadow; and there came a voice from the cloud, 'This is my Son, the Beloved. Listen to him.' Then suddenly, when they looked round, they saw no one with them any more but only Jesus.

As they came down the mountain he warned them to tell no one what they had seen, until after the Son of Man had risen from the dead. They observed the warning faithfully, though among themselves they discussed what 'rising from the dead' could mean.

The Transfiguration

As the time of the Passion approaches, the foreboding of the disciples grows. Jesus sustains them by this vivid experience of his more-than-natural nature. On the holy mountain of revelation they see him transformed. It was a real visual experience, though described in symbols familiar from the Bible, brilliant white clothes and so on. Moses and Elijah are seen there because they also had experienced the vision of God on the holy mountain. For Moses this was at the giving of the Law on Mount Sinai, for Elijah in the cave of Mount Horeb. The disciples were frightened, confused and overcome at the awesome experience, and yet comforted in a way which made Peter want to prolong it. This will later be the rare reaction of Christian mystics, a reassuring terror and a frightening homeliness, the awareness of a presence which is at the same time awesome and comforting, an experience which cannot fully be put into words. The Voice from Heaven is an echo of the Voice at Jesus's Baptism. There, however, it was addressed to Jesus, whereas here it is spoken to the disciples, proclaiming Jesus as authorised teacher, the extension of that same divine Voice.

Question: Is fear the right attitude we should have to God?

Just before the Jewish Passover Jesus went up to Jerusalem, and in the Temple he found people selling cattle and sheep and pigeons, and the money changers sitting at their counters there. Making a whip out of some cord, he drove them all out of the Temple, cattle and sheep as well, scattered the money changers' coins, knocked their tables over and said to the pigeon-sellers, 'Take all this out of here and stop turning my Father's house into a market.' Then his disciples remembered the words of scripture: Zeal for your house will devour me. The Jews intervened and said, 'What sign can you show us to justify what you have done?' Jesus answered, 'Destroy this sanctuary, and in three days I will raise it up.' The Jews replied, 'It has taken forty-six years to build this sanctuary: are you going to raise it up in three days?' But he was speaking of the sanctuary that was his body, and when Jesus rose from the dead, his disciples remembered that he had said this, and they believed the scripture and the words he had said.

During his stay in Jerusalem for the Passover many believed in his name when they saw the signs that he gave, but Jesus knew them all and did not trust himself to them; he never needed evidence about any man; he could tell what a man had in him.

The Cleansing of the Temple

According to John, this scene took place at the beginning of Jesus's ministry, on the first of Jesus's four visits to Jerusalem. At each subsequent visit the Temple authorities lay in wait for Jesus, increasingly keen to eliminate him, but unable to do so till his Hour had come. The other gospels place as the final climax both this incident and all other scenes of Jesus in Jerusalem. Whichever is correct, the incident is the basic cause of Jesus's arrest and tortured death. By his action Jesus had demonstrated that the worship carried out in the Temple was vain in God's eyes and must be superseded. To the Temple authorities this was intolerable, and he must be removed. Again, Jesus demanded a complete reversal of standards. His puzzling saying about building the Temple anew in his body was at last understood by his disciples to mean the Temple that was his Body, the Church. The material building which had been the centre of worship was no longer important. Henceforth all worship would occur in any place, but within the Christian community. The community – or the Church – was now the place of sanctification and of prayer to God.

Question: What was Jesus trying to show by his demonstration in the Temple?

Jesus said to Nicodemus:

'The Son of Man must be lifted up
as Moses lifted up the serpent in the desert,
so that everyone who believes may have eternal life
    in him.
Yes, God loved the world so much
that he gave his only Son,
so that everyone who believes in him may not be lost
but may have eternal life.
For God sent his Son into the world
not to condemn the world,
but so that through him the world might be saved.
No one who believes in him will be condemned;
but whoever refuses to believe is condemned already,
because he has refused to believe
in the name of God's only Son.
On these grounds is sentence pronounced:
that though the light has come into the world
men have shown they prefer
darkness to the light
because their deeds were evil.
And indeed, everybody who does wrong
hates the light and avoids it,
for fear his actions should be exposed;
but the man who lives by the truth
comes out into the light,
so that it may be plainly seen that what he does
    is done in God.'

Nicodemus

After Jesus's conversation with Nicodemus comes this reflection on his visit. Is it Jesus's reflection or the evangelist's? The text does not make it clear. Throughout the Gospel of John people are coming to Jesus and judging themselves by their reactions to Jesus. The Father judges no one, but has given all judgement to the Son. In his turn, the Son does not judge, but we judge ourselves by our reaction to him. So at the wedding at Cana the disciples believe in him and see his glory. In the Temple the Jews refuse belief and are condemned. Then comes Nicodemus in secret and in fear. He is sitting on the fence, afraid of the Pharisees, but by the time of the burial he has decided for Jesus. After Nicodemus comes the Samaritan woman, cheeky and unbelieving at first, but won over by Jesus's playful persistence. And so on: the Jews on one side, the man healed at the Pool of Bethzatha on the other; the Jews on one side, the man blind from birth on the other. The decision is ours too: when confronted by Jesus do we come to the light that our deeds may be known, or do we shun the light?

Question: How can we be afraid of the light?

Among those who went up to worship at the festival were some Greeks. These approached Philip, who came from Bethsaida in Galilee, and put this request to him, 'Sir, we should like to see Jesus.' Philip went to tell Andrew, and Andrew and Philip together went to tell Jesus. Jesus replied to them:

'Now the hour has come
for the Son of Man to be glorified.
I tell you, most solemnly,
unless a wheat grain falls on the ground
    and dies,
it remains only a single grain;
but if it dies,
it yields a rich harvest.
Anyone who loves his life loses it;
anyone who hates his life in this world
will keep it for the eternal life.
If a man serves me, he must follow me,
wherever I am, my servant will be there too.
If anyone serves me, my Father will honour him.
Now my soul is troubled.
What shall I say:
Father, save me from this hour?
But it was for this very reason that I have come
    to this hour.
Father, glorify your name!'

A voice came from heaven, 'I have glorified it, and I will glorify it again.' People standing by, who heard this, said it was a clap of thunder; others said, 'It was an angel speaking to him.' Jesus answered, 'It was not for my sake that this voice came, but for yours.

'Now sentence is being passed on this world;
now the prince of this world is to be overthrown.
And when I am lifted up from the earth,
I shall draw all men to myself.'

By these words he indicated the kind of death he would die.

Exaltation through Suffering

This moving gospel reading is the immediate prelude to the account of the Last Supper and the Passion. It is full of Jesus's dread and confidence at what he knows is approaching. In the Gospel of John there is no agony in the garden before Jesus's arrest, for in John the story of the Passion is so shaped that it is clearly the triumph of the Son of Man. There is no mention of humiliation or mockery. Jesus remains in control from the beginning, when he permits the guards to take him into custody, till the end, when he calls out that he is ready to die, 'It is complete'. This is all the hour of the exaltation of the Son of Man, when Jesus is raised up in every sense. All the more important, then, for John to show before the Passion that the cost for Jesus was real, with this little dialogue in prayer between Jesus and his Father. This is John's equivalent of the prayer in the garden. Today's second reading, from Hebrews, shows that there were in early Christianity strong but slightly variant traditions of Jesus's prayer before his Passion. All express his very human fear, his unshakable commitment to his task and his loving confidence in his Father's care.

Question: What are my real fears? Can I entrust them to God?

The Passion of Our Lord Jesus Christ According to Mark

First thing in the morning, the chief priest together with the elders and scribes, in short the whole Sanhedrin, had their plan ready. They had Jesus bound and took him away and handed him over to Pilate.

Pilate questioned him, 'Are you the king of the Jews?' 'It is you who say it' he answered. And the chief priests brought many accusations against him. Pilate questioned him again, 'Have you no reply at all? See how many accusations they are bringing against you!' But, to Pilate's amazement, Jesus made no further reply.

At festival time Pilate used to release a prisoner for them, anyone they asked for. Now a man called Barabbas was then in prison with the rioters who had committed murder during the uprising. When the crowd went up and began to ask Pilate the customary favour, Pilate answered them, 'Do you want me to release for you the king of the Jews?' For he realised it was out of jealousy that the chief priests had handed Jesus over. The chief priests, however, had incited the crowd to demand that he should release Barabbas for them instead. Then

Pilate spoke again. 'But in that case, what am I to do with the man you call king of the Jews?' They shouted back, 'Crucify him!' 'Why?' Pilate asked them 'What harm has he done?' But they shouted all the louder, 'Crucify him!' So Pilate, anxious to placate the crowd, released Barabbas for them and, having ordered Jesus to be scourged, handed him over to be crucified.

The soldiers led him away to the inner part of the palace, that is, the Praetorium, and called the whole cohort together. They dressed him up in purple, twisted some thorns into a crown and put it on him. And they began saluting him, 'Hail, king of the Jews!' They struck his head with a reed and spat on him; and they went down on their knees to do him homage. And when they had finished making fun of him, they took off the purple and dressed him in his own clothes.

They led him out to crucify him. They enlisted a passer-by, Simon of Cyrene, father of Alexander and Rufus, who was coming in from the country, to carry his cross. They brought Jesus to the place called Golgotha, which means the place of the skull.

They offered him wine mixed with myrrh, but he refused it. Then they crucified him, and shared out his clothing, casting lots to decide what each should get. It was the third hour when they crucified him. The inscription giving the charge against him read: 'The King of the Jews.' And they crucified two robbers with him, one on his right and one on his left.

The passers-by jeered at him; they shook their heads and said, 'Aha! So you would destroy the Temple and rebuild it in three days! Then save yourself: come down from the cross!' The chief priests and the scribes mocked him among themselves in the same way. 'He saved others,' they said 'he cannot save himself. Let the Christ, the king of Israel, come down from the cross now, for us to see it and believe.' Even those who were crucified with him taunted him.

When the sixth hour came there was darkness over the whole land until the ninth hour. And at the ninth hour Jesus cried out in a loud voice, 'Eloi, Eloi, lama sabachthani?' which means 'My God, my God, why have you deserted me?' When some of those who stood by heard this, they said, 'Listen, he is calling on Elijah.' Someone ran and soaked a sponge in vinegar and, putting it on a reed, gave it him to drink saying, 'Wait and see if Elijah will come to take him down.' But Jesus gave a loud cry and breathed his last. And the veil of the Temple was torn in two from top to bottom. The centurion, who was standing in front of him, had seen how he had died, and he said, 'In truth this man was a son of God.'

(Longer form, Mark 14:1-15:47)

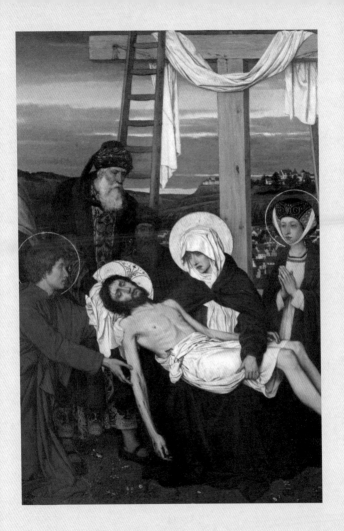

The Passion According to Mark

1. Jesus deserted

The Gospel of Mark is concerned to show Jesus as a real, human person. So the story of the Passion begins with the very real fear and horror of Jesus in the garden. Mark represents Jesus as almost beside himself with apprehension at the torture which he knew he would suffer. Again and again he returns to seek companionship from his disciples, to find them callously asleep. The Passion-story ends, too, with a loud cry of agony as Jesus breathes his last.

2. The divine Jesus

The core of the Passion-story is the trial scene. Before the high priest, Jesus acknowledges that he is the Messiah of Judaism, and the Son of the Blessed One. To these titles he joins 'Son of Man'. In the Book of Daniel the Son of Man is a glorious figure who triumphs over persecution to receive from God all power on earth. So now Jesus claims to share God's throne as that Son of Man. It is for these divine claims that he is rejected as a blasphemer and handed over to the Romans.

3. The triumph of God

When Jesus cries out on the cross 'My God, my God, why have you deserted me?', he is not in despair, but is beginning Psalm 22. The Psalm begins in persecution, but ends in the triumph of God and the vindication of the sufferer. This gives the meaning of his Passion: by it Jesus brings the triumph of God and his own vindication by God. The Cross is the moment, not of abandonment by God, but of the most complete union of Jesus to the Father. Jesus here establishes the Sovereignty of his Father by his total, loving obedience. This is why the centurion proclaims, 'In truth, this man was a son of God.' It is also significant that here for the first time in the gospels a human being recognises Jesus as Son of God. It is not a Jew but a gentile – the beginning of the spread of the gospel to all nations of the world.

It was very early on the first day of the week and still dark, when Mary of Magdala came to the tomb. She saw that the stone had been moved away from the tomb and came running to Simon Peter and the other disciple, the one Jesus loved. 'They have taken the Lord out of the tomb' she said 'and we don't know where they have put him.'

So Peter set out with the other disciple to go to the tomb. They ran together, but the other disciple, running faster than Peter, reached the tomb first; he bent down and saw the linen cloths lying on the ground, but did not go in. Simon Peter who was following now came up, went right into the tomb, saw the linen cloths on the ground, and also the cloth that had been over his head; this was not with the linen cloths but rolled up in a place by itself. Then the other disciple who had reached the tomb first also went in; he saw and he believed. Till this moment they had failed to understand the teaching of scripture, that he must rise from the dead.

The Empty Tomb

There are several accounts in the various gospels of the discovery of the empty tomb. The slight variations between them show all the marks of oral tradition, for in genuine oral tradition each 'performance' is different. Different people tell the story slightly differently, stressing different aspects. This story stresses the proof that the tomb really was empty, for the apostles examine the evidence carefully. Other accounts concentrate less on the evidence and more on the message, that they will meet the Risen Lord in Galilee. It was important to establish that the tomb was empty, to prevent the charge that the meetings with the Risen Christ were simply ghost-appearances. Apart from the proof that this was a real, living and bodily person, these meetings stress two factors, the power of the Risen Christ and the commission given to the disciples. They are to go out into the whole world and spread the message, always accompanied by and strengthened by Christ himself. In this account Simon Peter is clearly the senior, authority figure, to whom the Beloved Disciple defers. But it is the love of the Beloved Disciple which immediately brings him to faith.

Question: Is the empty tomb the chief evidence for the Resurrection?

In the evening of that same day, the first day of the week, the doors were closed in the room where the disciples were, for fear of the Jews. Jesus came and stood among them. He said to them 'Peace be with you', and showed them his hands and his side. The disciples were filled with joy when they saw the Lord, and he said to them again,

'Peace be with you.
As the Father sent me,
so am I sending you.'

After saying this he breathed on them and said:

'Receive the Holy Spirit.
For those whose sins you forgive,
they are forgiven;
for those whose sins you retain,
they are retained.'

Thomas, called the Twin, who was one of the Twelve, was not with them when Jesus came. When the disciples said, 'We have seen the Lord', he answered, 'Unless I see the holes that the nails made in his hands and can put my finger into the holes they made, and unless I can put my hand into his side, I refuse to believe.' Eight days later the disciples were in the house again and Thomas was with them. The doors were closed, but Jesus came in and stood among them. 'Peace be with you,' he said. Then he spoke to Thomas, 'Put your finger here; look, here are my hands. Give me your hand; put it into my side. Doubt no longer but believe.' Thomas replied, 'My Lord and my God!'

Jesus said to him:

> 'You believe because you can see me.
> Happy are those who have not seen
> and yet believe.'

There were many other signs that Jesus worked and the disciples saw, but they are not recorded in this book. These are recorded so that you may believe that Jesus is the Christ, the Son of God, and that believing this you may have life through his name.

Jesus in the Upper Room

Two aspects of this meeting are especially striking. This is the last scene of the Gospel of John, for chapter 21 is an appendix. At the end, before the concluding reflection, Thomas gives the only direct acclamation in the New Testament of Jesus as God. Nowhere else is Jesus directly hailed as 'God', though there are ways in which he is equivalently so presented. So, in a way, this acclamation of the Risen Christ is the climax of the New Testament. Secondly, it is striking that Jesus's final blessing is of peace and forgiveness. The mission of all Christians is to bring these to a troubled world. Throughout the Bible, God is a God of forgiveness. The Old Testament consists of a series of covenants of forgiveness, each in turn broken by God's chosen people – the covenant with Noah after the Flood, the covenant with Abraham, with Moses after the worship of the Golden Calf, finally the new covenant promised by Jeremiah when unfaithful Israel is being exiled to Babylon. Christianity is not for the perfect but for the sinner, surrounded by sinners. Forgiven sinners must bring forgiveness to all those around them.

Question: How far is the authority of the Church compatible with individual judgement?

The disciples told their story of what had happened on the road and how they had recognised Jesus at the breaking of bread.

They were still talking about this when Jesus himself stood among them and said to them, 'Peace be with you!' In a state of alarm and fright, they thought they were seeing a ghost. But he said, 'Why are you so agitated, and why are these doubts rising in your hearts? Look at my hands and feet; yes, it is I indeed. Touch me and see for yourselves; a ghost has no flesh and bones as you can see I have.' And as he said this he showed them his hands and feet. Their joy was so great that they could not believe it, and they stood there dumbfounded; so he said to them, 'Have you anything here to eat?' And they offered him a piece of grilled fish, which he took and ate before their eyes.

Then he told them, 'This is what I meant when I said, while I was still with you, that everything written about me in the Law of Moses, in the Prophets and in the Psalms, has to be fulfilled.' He then opened their minds to understand the scriptures, and he said to them, 'So you see how it is written that the Christ would suffer and on the third day rise from the dead, and that, in his name, repentance for the forgiveness of sins would be preached to all the nations, beginning from Jerusalem. You are witnesses to this.'

Fish for Supper

The two disciples had met Jesus on their way to Emmaus. There Jesus had used the Eucharistic meal to reveal himself to them, for the Eucharist is always an occasion for us to get to know the Risen Christ better. Now he meets the whole group of disciples in their refuge, the Upper Room. It is perhaps the same incident as we heard last Sunday, but with different emphasis. Now the stress is on the meeting with a real person, not just a ghost. That is why he eats a piece of fish. The important lesson of this is that, in our resurrection to true life, it is the whole person that is raised, not just the soul. Christian teaching is that a person is an animated body. We work out our salvation with fingers and toes and other bodily members, and all will be raised to life. It is not just a matter of thoughts and intentions! The whole body is baptised into Christ and is the instrument of our salvation. The body will be changed, and St Paul tells us that it is stupid to ask what sort of body we will have in the resurrection, but we will be raised as a whole person.

Question: Will we have bodies in heaven?

Jesus said:

'I am the good shepherd:
the good shepherd is one who lays down his life
    for his sheep.
The hired man, since he is not the shepherd
and the sheep do not belong to him,
abandons the sheep and runs away
as soon as he sees a wolf coming,
and then the wolf attacks and scatters the sheep;
this is because he is only a hired man
and has no concern for the sheep.
I am the good shepherd;
I know my own and my own know me,
just as the Father knows me and I know the Father;
and I lay down my life for my sheep.
And there are other sheep I have
that are not of this fold,
and these I have to lead as well.
They too will listen to my voice,
and there will be only one flock,
and one shepherd.
The Father loves me,
because I lay down my life
in order to take it up again.
No one takes it from me;
I lay it down of my own free will,
and as it is in my power to lay it down,
so it is in my power to take it up again;
and this is the command I have been given
    by my Father.'

The Good Shepherd

Each year on this Sunday there is a reading from John about the Good Shepherd. To think of ourselves as woolly and cuddly sheep, obedient to the shepherd, would be a mistake. Sheep are renowned as being silly, contradictory creatures, always starting off in the wrong direction, getting themselves into tangles and difficulties. In the Holy Land they are scraggy beasts, pastured on rocky and often dangerous ground, amid boulders and rocky cliffs, threatened by wild animals and marauders. It was not simply a matter of the shepherd sitting on a rock and idly playing his pipe. He needed to be on the alert to save the sheep from hurting themselves. So Jesus as the good shepherd is kept well occupied by our foibles, our stubbornness, our mistakes and our fears. Again, as in today's other two readings, there is the reassurance of a close relationship with the Father. Jesus knows us intimately, just as he knows the Father. It is questionable whether in real life a shepherd should lay down his life for his sheep: what would happen to the remainder of the flock? But it is an expression of his whole-hearted devotion to the sheep, and an assimilation to the case of Jesus.

Question: Are you a sheep?

Jesus said to his disciples:
'I am the true vine,
and my Father is the vinedresser.
Every branch in me that bears no fruit
he cuts away,
and every branch that does bear fruit he prunes
to make it bear even more.
You are pruned already,
by means of the word that I have spoken to you.
Make your home in me, as I make mine in you.
As a branch cannot bear fruit all by itself,
but must remain part of the vine,
neither can you unless you remain in me.
I am the vine,
you are the branches.
Whoever remains in me, with me in him,
bears fruit in plenty;
for cut off from me you can do nothing.
Anyone who does not remain in me
is like a branch that has been thrown away
– he withers;
these branches are collected and thrown on the fire,
and they are burnt.
If you remain in me
and my words remain in you,
you may ask what you will
and you shall get it.
It is to the glory of my Father that you should
   bear much fruit,
and then you will be my disciples.'

The True Vine

A vine is an extraordinary plant. It can grow to a huge size, spreading over a huge area, a whole garden wall or trellis-work, from one single root, and producing a rich sap which yields grapes at the end of countless little branches. And then there is the business of pruning: cut it back thoroughly on all its many shoots and tendrils, and it seems only more determined to grow thick and strong. So the vine was the symbol of Israel, drawing from the Lord a sap which penetrated to all its shoots, and lovingly pruned by the gardener in a way which best encouraged its growth. The image was taken over by Jesus for his own community, the new Israel. Pairing with last week's picture of the good shepherd, it is one of the greatest of John's images. It perfectly sums up the two emphases of today's other two readings. The only source of fruitful energy for the Christian is union with and dependence on the life flowing from Christ. Without that, the branches wither and die; a trimming cut off from a vine no longer has any chance of life. The vine itself at pruning season looks stark, rough and suffering. It is in fact bursting with new life.

Question: Have I benefited from the vinedresser's pruning knife?

JOHN 15:9-17

Jesus said to his disciples:
   'As the Father has loved me,
   so I have loved you.
   Remain in my love.
   If you keep my commandments
   you will remain in my love,
   just as I have kept my Father's commandments
   and remain in his love.
   I have told you this
   so that my own joy may be in you
   and your joy be complete.
   This is my commandment:
   love one another, as I have loved you.
   A man can have no greater love
   than to lay down his life for his friends.
   You are my friends,
   if you do what I command you.
   I shall not call you servants any more,
   because a servant does not know
   his master's business;
   I call you friends,
   because I have made known to you
   everything I have learnt from my Father.
   You did not choose me, no, I chose you;
   and I commissioned you
   to go out and to bear fruit,
   fruit that will last;
   and then the Father will give you
   anything you ask him in my name.
   What I command you is to love one another.'

The Father's Love

Like so many of the great discourses of Jesus in the Gospel of John, these are not a shorthand record of Jesus's words, but will have been written up afterwards. Most probably there were several slightly different versions of what Jesus said at the Last Supper. In any case, one can see that the author has in mind two different levels, both Jesus's own historical situation at the Last Supper and the situation of the early Church, where the disciples are being hard put to the test in their mission. They need encouraging by Jesus's own example of his sacrifice and by his promise of real friendship: they are friends, not servants, specially chosen by Jesus to bear fruit that will last. So we too are welcomed as friends, chosen and commissioned by Jesus to go out and bear fruit, but reminded that we must be prepared to pay the price. There is no fruit without pruning. Jesus had just given the example of service by washing the feet of his disciples. If we are to share the joy of Jesus we must be ready to join him also in laying down his life for his friends.

Question: Do we ever have to make hard choices for Christ?

Jesus showed himself to the Eleven, and said to them, 'Go out to the whole world; proclaim the Good News to all creation. He who believes and is baptised will be saved; he who does not believe will be condemned. These are the signs that will be associated with believers: in my name they will cast out devils; they will have the gift of tongues; they will pick up snakes in their hands, and be unharmed should they drink deadly poison; they will lay their hands on the sick, who will recover.'

And so the Lord Jesus, after he had spoken to them, was taken up into heaven: there at the right hand of God he took his place, while they, going out, preached everywhere, the Lord working with them and confirming the word by the signs that accompanied it.

The Conclusion of the Gospel of Mark

This final blessing on the mission of the disciples summarises events narrated in the Acts of the Apostles, events which show the power of the Spirit at work in their mission. Finally the account of the Ascension itself is given, modelled on the account given in the Acts, the assurance of the power of Christ which stands behind all the works of his followers and believers. Most of these activities would not be expected in today's Church, but the first and the last are still the task of the Church. Casting out evil spirits and healing may not be done so dramatically as in the gospel miracles, but it is still the Christian's task to bring goodness where there is evil and healing where there are wounds. We have many opportunities in the course of the day either to foment or to soothe anger and enmity, to roughen a wound or to smooth it down. As we know from our failures to do this, such works are the works of the Spirit of Christ, supporting our own weakness and triumphing over our own leanings towards evil.

Question: What would you say are the marks of Christ's presence and power at work in the Church?

Jesus said to his disciples:
  'When the Advocate comes,
  whom I shall send to you from the Father,
  the Spirit of truth who issues from the Father,
  he will be my witness.
  And you too will be witnesses,
  because you have been with me from the outset.

  I still have many things to say to you
  but they would be too much for you now.
  But when the Spirit of truth comes
  he will lead you to the complete truth,
  since he will not be speaking as from himself
  but will say only what he has learnt,
  and he will tell you of the things to come.
  He will glorify me,
  since all he tells you
  will be taken from what is mine.
  Everything the Father has is mine;
  that is why I said:
  All he tells you
  will be taken from what is mine.'

The Advocate

In Jesus's final instructions to his disciples, gathered together at the Last Supper, he gives them four little promises about the Advocate whom he will send, send from the Father. 'Advocate' is really a legal term, in both English and the original Greek, and the Spirit will 'testify' on behalf of Jesus. The certainty and definitiveness of this terminology is important. In other sayings Jesus promises that the Advocate will lead his disciples into all truth, enabling them to understand what they cannot yet grasp. With these promises, therefore, we are celebrating the continuing presence of the Spirit, leading the Church into all truth, into a continuously fuller and more profound understanding of the mystery of Christ. It is through the Spirit that, under the guidance of the Church, each generation and culture is enabled to assimilate and express – sometimes with a wobble or two – the great truths in its own terms, each generation building on the truths perceived by previous guidance. There must be a constant renewal in our personal understanding, under the guidance and testimony of this Advocate speaking through the Church. The Advocate guides our minds, but above all the mind of the teaching Church.

Question: What aspect of Christian teaching is the Spirit stressing to us in these days?

The eleven disciples set out for Galilee, to the mountain where Jesus had arranged to meet them. When they saw him they fell down before him, though some hesitated. Jesus came up and spoke to them. He said, 'All authority in heaven and on earth has been given to me. Go, therefore, make disciples of all the nations; baptise them in the name of the Father and of the Son and of the Holy Spirit, and teach them to observe all the commands I gave you. And know that I am with you always; yes, to the end of time.'

THE MOST HOLY TRINITY

Baptism into the Trinity

On a superficial level this gospel reading seems chosen because of the Trinitarian baptismal formula. It is the only time this formula comes in the scripture, and it is remarkable that the Trinitarian liturgical formula was already developed while the New Testament was being written. At a deeper level this reading of the final five verses of Matthew gives a wonderful Trinitarian view of the work of salvation. The words of the Risen Christ, 'all authority in heaven and on earth has been given to me', are reminiscent of the vision of the exalted Son of Man in Daniel, who comes to the One of Great Age, seated on his throne, and receives from him all power on earth. Only Christ receives all power in heaven too, as 'the Son of God in power'. In this power he sends out his disciples, promising his divine presence always. The promise of Christ's divine presence in his Church now, at the end of the Gospel, balances the promise at the beginning in the name Emmanuel, given by the angel for the child. Emmanuel means 'God with us'. So the permanent presence of Christ is the message of the whole Gospel.

Question: If Christ is present in his Church, why is it so sinful?

MARK 14:12-16, 22-26

On the first day of Unleavened Bread, when the Passover lamb was sacrificed, his disciples said to Jesus, 'Where do you want us to go and make the preparations for you to eat the Passover?' So he sent two of his disciples, saying to them, 'Go into the city and you will meet a man carrying a pitcher of water. Follow him, and say to the owner of the house which he enters, "The Master says: Where is my dining room in which I can eat the Passover with my disciples?" He will show you a large upper room furnished with couches, all prepared. Make the preparations for us there.' The disciples set out and went to the city and found everything as he had told them, and prepared the Passover.

And as they were eating he took some bread, and when he had said the blessing he broke it and gave it to them. 'Take it,' he said 'this is my body.' Then he took a cup, and when he had returned thanks he gave it to them, and all drank from it, and he said to them, 'This is my blood, the blood of the covenant, which is to be poured out for many. I tell you solemnly, I shall not drink any more wine until the day I drink the new wine in the kingdom of God.'

After psalms had been sung they left for the Mount of Olives.

A New Partnership

The original, Old Testament covenant was sealed by a death and by the sharing of the blood between God (signified by the altar) and his people as a sign of new life. Israel broke that covenant by persistently refusing to keep true to the way of life which the covenant enshrined. Now Jesus's new covenant engages us in a new alliance and gives us new life. The story told in this reading is the warranty and guarantee that, each time we receive the Body and Blood of Christ, we are bound anew into his covenant. The story is told in almost exactly similar terms in each of the first three gospels and in Paul's first letter to the Corinthians. It must have been learnt and repeated by heart. There is just enough difference to show that Mark and Matthew reflect the tradition of the Hebrew communities, while Paul and Luke reflect the tradition of the Greek-speaking communities. It must have been repeated again and again from the very first years of Christianity. Each time we repeat these words we are entering again into Jesus's covenant. There should be a health warning. The Mass is dangerous: are you ready to commit yourself to the Kingdom, to engage in a new and personal alliance with Christ and to live with his life?

Question: What obligations do we take on by receiving the Eucharist?

Jesus went home with his disciples, and such a crowd collected that they could not even have a meal. When his relatives heard of this, they set out to take charge of him, convinced he was out of his mind.

The scribes who had come down from Jerusalem were saying, 'Beelzebul is in him' and 'It is through the prince of devils that he casts devils out.' So he called them to him and spoke to them in parables, 'How can Satan cast out Satan? If a kingdom is divided against itself, that kingdom cannot last. And if a household is divided against itself, that household can never stand. Now if Satan has rebelled against himself and is divided, he cannot stand either – it is the end of him. But no one can make his way into a strong man's house and burgle his property unless he has tied up the strong man first. Only then can he burgle his house.

'I tell you solemnly, all men's sins will be forgiven, and all their blasphemies; but let anyone blaspheme against the Holy Spirit and he will never have forgiveness: he is guilty of an eternal sin.' This was because they were saying, 'An unclean spirit is in him.'

His mother and brothers now arrived and, standing outside, sent in a message asking for him. A crowd was sitting round him at the time the message was passed to him, 'Your mother and brothers and sisters are outside asking for you.' He replied, 'Who are my mother and my brothers?' And looking round at those sitting in a circle about him, he said, 'Here are my mother and my brothers. Anyone who does the will of God, that person is my brother and sister and mother.'

Jesus Rejected

The first stage of Jesus's ministry comes to an end. He is rejected as 'out of his mind' by his own family. Then he is rejected by the scribes as being in league with Beelzebul. Finally his family again arrive, looking for him, and he turns to those who are listening to him as his true family. This all leads into the Parable of the Sower, which seems to be Jesus's reflection on his rejection by most people, and his fruitful acceptance by a small number of disciples. It is, of course, significant that the scribes cannot deny that he drives out evil spirits. If even his enemies are forced to admit it, it must be true. The best they can do is sarcastically to ascribe his powers to the chief of evil spirits, here named 'Beelzebub' or 'Beelzebul' (two different versions of the text). The former name means 'lord of the flies', probably a mocking corruption of the latter, which means 'lord prince', the title of a local deity. The whole scene presents an agonising picture of the isolation of Jesus. In Luke's version of the scene, by a very slight adjustment, Jesus's mother and brothers are the prime example of those who hear the word of God and keep it.

Question: Did Jesus feel disappointment and isolation as we do?

Jesus said to the crowds: 'This is what the kingdom of God is like. A man throws seed on the land. Night and day, while he sleeps, when he is awake, the seed is sprouting and growing; how, he does not know. Of its own accord the land produces first the shoot, then the ear, then the full grain in the ear. And when the crop is ready, he loses no time: he starts to reap because the harvest has come.'

He also said, 'What can we say the kingdom of God is like? What parable can we find for it? It is like a mustard seed which at the time of its sowing in the soil is the smallest of all the seeds on earth; yet once it is sown it grows into the biggest shrub of them all and puts out big branches so that the birds of the air can shelter in its shade.'

Using many parables like these, he spoke the word to them, so far as they were capable of understanding it. He would not speak to them except in parables, but he explained everything to his disciples when they were alone.

The Seed Growing

Jesus was a countryman, from the rich agricultural plains of Galilee, where wheat and fruit trees abounded. It was natural for him to use such imagery for the Kingship of God which he was proclaiming. Today's gospel reading offers us two of the many images in Mark's chapter of parables. What did Jesus want to teach by them? Images can carry many layers of meaning. First, the Seed Growing Secretly. Perhaps Jesus meant that God's purposes are accomplished in spite of our feeble and fumbling efforts. Perhaps it was a warning that, after long waiting, the time for decision, the time of harvest, had come with Jesus's own mission. Then the Mustard Seed: was this a reply to the discouraged disciples – or perhaps Jesus's critical opponents – that his motley little group of undistinguished peasants, fishermen and tax-collectors would grow into God's own mighty tree. Perhaps this is a first hint that Jesus's mission is for all nations, not just for Israel. All nations would come, nest and find a home in its branches, just as in today's first reading they nest in the branches of the great cedar tree. At any rate, both images show that God is in charge, and has great plans which will be fulfilled despite our own inadequacies.

Question: What does Jesus mean to teach by this parable?

The time came for Elizabeth to have her child, and she gave birth to a son; and when her neighbours and relations heard that the Lord had shown her so great a kindness, they shared her joy.

Now on the eighth day they came to circumcise the child; they were going to call him Zechariah after his father, but his mother spoke up. 'No,' she said 'he is to be called John.' They said to her, 'But no one in your family has that name', and made signs to his father to find out what he wanted him called. The father asked for a writing-tablet and wrote, 'His name is John.' And they were all astonished. At that instant his power of speech returned and he spoke and praised God. All their neighbours were filled with awe and the whole affair was talked about throughout the hill country of Judaea. All those who heard of it treasured it in their hearts. 'What will this child turn out to be?' they wondered. And indeed the hand of the Lord was with him. Meanwhile, the child grew up and his spirit matured. And he lived out in the wilderness until the day he appeared openly to Israel.

The Birth and Naming of John the Baptist

The birth-stories of John the Baptist and of Jesus are told in such a way as to bring out the parallelism between the two figures, and the special position of each. Of each, the parents are models of the fidelity of Israel, and of trust in the Lord. An angel foretells the miraculous birth of each. The birth and naming of each is an occasion of great joy. In each case John is great but Jesus is greater still: the exalted position of John serves to exalt the position of Jesus even further. John will prepare the way; Jesus will be seated on the throne of his father David. Zechariah doubts and is struck dumb; Mary humbly enquires and is blessed. John's name means 'God is gracious', Jesus's name is 'Saviour'. At the birth of John there is joy in the family, at the birth of Jesus the joy and singing are by the angels. At the end of this passage John goes out into the desert because it was from the desert that the Messiah was expected to come, and John will be the herald voice, crying in the desert in fulfilment of Isaiah, 'Make straight his paths.'

Question: What would you have advised John the Baptist to do in the desert?

When Jesus had crossed in the boat to the other side, a large crowd gathered round him and he stayed by the lakeside. Then one of the synagogue officials came up, Jairus by name, and seeing him, fell at his feet and pleaded with him earnestly, saying, 'My little daughter is desperately sick. Do come and lay your hands on her to make her better and save her life.' Jesus went with him and a large crowd followed him; they were pressing all round him.

Now there was a woman who had suffered from a haemorrhage for twelve years; after long and painful treatment under various doctors, she had spent all she had without being any the better for it, in fact, she was getting worse. She had heard about Jesus, and she came up behind him through the crowd and touched his cloak. 'If I can touch even his clothes,' she had told herself 'I shall be well again.' And the source of the bleeding dried up instantly, and she felt in herself that she was cured of her complaint. Immediately aware that power had gone out from him Jesus turned round in the crowd and said, 'Who touched my clothes?'

His disciples said to him, 'You see how the crowd is pressing round you and yet you say, "Who touched me?"' But he continued to look all round to see who had done it. Then the woman came forward, frightened and trembling because she knew what had happened to her, and she fell at his feet and told him the whole truth. 'My daughter,' he said 'your faith has restored you to health; go in peace and be free from your complaint.'

While he was still speaking some people arrived from the house of the synagogue official to say, 'Your daughter is dead: why put the Master to any further trouble?' But Jesus had overheard this remark of theirs and he said to the official, 'Do not be afraid; only have faith.' And he allowed no one to go with him except Peter and James and John the brother of James.

So they came to the official's house and Jesus noticed all the commotion, with people weeping and wailing unrestrainedly. He went in and said to them, 'Why all this commotion and crying? The child is not dead, but asleep.' But they laughed at him. So he turned them all out and, taking with him the child's father and mother and his own companions, he went into the place where the child lay. And taking the child by the hand he said to her, 'Talitha, kum!' which means, 'Little girl, I tell you to get up.'

The little girl got up at once and began to walk about, for she was twelve years old. At this they were overcome with astonishment, and he ordered them strictly not to let anyone know about it, and told them to give her something to eat.

Two Cures of Women

The author of the Gospel of Mark likes to combine incidents to show their joint significance, often, as here, sandwiching one story between the two halves of another. In this instance the significance is surely that both recipients of Jesus's healing love are women. Only a minority of Jesus's miracles concern women, and the bringing together of these two, one a girl and the other an old woman, serves to stress their importance to Jesus. It is unfair to accuse the Bible of being male-dominated. A mother's devotion is a frequent image of God's love. There are plenty of feisty women in the Old Testament, who put their menfolk to shame by their courage, enterprise and initiative: Rebecca, Tamar, Deborah, Ruth, Esther, Judith. Jesus's own relationships with women seem to have been easy and even humorous. One need only think of his playful bargaining with the Syro-Phoenician over the cure of her daughter, or the jokey exchange between Jesus and the Samaritan woman at the well, not to mention his delicacy towards the woman taken in adultery or the sinful woman who showed her love by weeping at his feet. Paul also clearly relied in many ways in his apostolate on the ministry of women.

Question: What is Jesus's attitude to women? Is the Church fair to women?

Jesus went to his home town and his disciples accompanied him. With the coming of the sabbath he began teaching in the synagogue and most of them were astonished when they heard him. They said, 'Where did the man get all this? What is this wisdom that has been granted him, and these miracles that are worked through him? This is the carpenter, surely, the son of Mary, the brother of James and Joset and Jude and Simon? His sisters, too are they not here with us?' And they would not accept him. And Jesus said to them, 'A prophet is only despised in his own country among his own relations and in his own house'; and he could work no miracle there, though he cured a few sick people by laying his hands on them. He was amazed at their lack of faith.

FOURTEENTH SUNDAY IN ORDINARY TIME

A Visit to Nazareth

The very last sentence of the reading speaks of their lack
of faith. What was this lack of faith? They recognised in
Jesus an extraordinary wisdom and a power of miracles,
but this seems not to have been enough. What more
was needed? Faith is not the acceptance of a set of
propositions, 'I believe that the earth circles the sun',
etc. It is putting all my trust in God as my only hope.
Abraham, the model of faith, went out into the desert,
leaving everything on which he relied, everything that
made him what he was. He even trusted God to get him
out of the unbearable fix when God told him to sacrifice
his only son. The townsfolk of Nazareth presumably
thought they knew Jesus through and through. They were
prepared to acknowledge his wisdom and his miracles.
But they were not prepared to go further and see that God
was at work in him, that he was the manifestation of God
among them. It is all very well to admire Jesus, to think
him a fine teacher and a heroic, honourable man, who
gave everything for his high ideals; but unless we see God
in him, the divine transcendence of all that is human, he
cannot work the miracle of taking us to himself.

Question: Would Jesus have been hurt by their failure
to recognise him? How was it that they did not react
more favourably?

Jesus summoned the Twelve and began to send them out in pairs giving them authority over the unclean spirits. And he instructed them to take nothing for the journey except a staff – no bread, no haversack, no coppers for their purses. They were to wear sandals but, he added, 'Do not take a spare tunic.' And he said to them, 'If you enter a house anywhere, stay there until you leave the district. And if any place does not welcome you and people refuse to listen to you, as you walk away shake off the dust from under your feet as a sign to them.' So they set off to preach repentance; and they cast out many devils, and anointed many sick people with oil and cured them.

Instructions for Missioners

The instructions for missioners are shaped by the urgency of the Kingdom. They are to travel light for speed. They should wear sandals rather than go barefoot, also for speed and security. They are to rely for their provisions on the welcome they receive, and if they are unwelcome, they should not waste time on those who reject them. Did Jesus think that the Kingdom or Kingship of God would finally burst on the world in his own time, that there was so little time to spare? In one way it did – at his death and Resurrection, which fulfilled God's plan and restored us to friendship with God. In another way it is still in the future: the reign of peace and justice is not yet established. There is still sorrow, distress, enmity, fraud, jealousy and plenty of other evils which fracture God's Kingship. We are still imperfect reflections of the light of Christ, still pilgrim members of a pilgrim Church. Our efforts are feeble, even in Christ's footsteps. We cannot sit back complacently, any more than the missioners of Jesus's own time, and the task of establishing the Kingdom is still imminent.

Question: How can missioners best bring Christ's light and God's joy to the world?

The apostles rejoined Jesus and told him all they had done and taught. Then he said to them, 'You must come away to some lonely place all by yourselves and rest for a while'; for there were so many coming and going that the apostles had no time even to eat. So they went off in a boat to a lonely place where they could be by themselves. But people saw them going, and many could guess where; and from every town they all hurried to the place on foot and reached it before them. So as he stepped ashore he saw a large crowd; and he took pity on them because they were like sheep without a shepherd, and he set himself to teach them at some length.

The Feeding of the Five Thousand

This account introduces a series of six Sunday gospels on the Eucharist. As this year's gospel, Mark, is too short to provide readings for the whole year, it is after this account of the Feeding in Mark that the Church moves on to insert five Sundays of John's Bread of Life discourse. The story can be read on several levels. It is a foretaste of the Eucharist, the disciples gathered round Jesus as the new Israel (twelve baskets for the twelve tribes) for a fully satisfying meal, the messianic banquet. Jesus is the good shepherd who feeds his flock, according to Psalm 23, on the green pastures beside the restful waters of the Lake of Galilee. Jesus is the prophet, like Moses, who provides manna for his people in the desert, or more exactly like Elisha in 2 Kings 4 (next Sunday's first reading). The story is recounted in terms which deliberately recall these and other biblical scenes, concentrating more on the meaning than on the historical facts. There must, of course, have been a wonderful feeding at the base of the story, but it is difficult to re-establish exactly what this was.

Question: Would you say this meal was a Eucharist or not?

JOHN 6:1-15

Jesus went off to the other side of the Sea of Galilee – or of Tiberias – and a large crowd followed him, impressed by the signs he gave by curing the sick. Jesus climbed the hillside, and sat down there with his disciples. It was shortly before the Jewish feast of Passover.

Looking up, Jesus saw the crowds approaching and said to Philip, 'Where can we buy some bread for these people to eat?' He only said this to test Philip; he himself knew exactly what he was going to do. Philip answered, 'Two hundred denarii would only buy enough to give them a small piece each.' One of his disciples, Andrew, Simon Peter's brother, said, 'There is a small boy here with five barley loaves and two fish; but what is that between so many?' Jesus said to them, 'Make the people sit down.' There was plenty of grass there, and as many as five thousand men sat down. Then Jesus took the loaves, gave thanks, and gave them out to all who were sitting ready; he then did the same with the fish, giving out as much as was wanted. When they had eaten enough he said to the disciples, 'Pick up the pieces left over, so that nothing gets wasted.' So they picked them up, and filled twelve hampers with scraps left over from the meal of five barley loaves. The people, seeing this sign that he had given, said, 'This really is the prophet who is to come into the world.' Jesus, who could see they were about to come and take him by force and make him king, escaped back to the hills by himself.

The Feeding of the Five Thousand

Just like Mark's story (last Sunday's gospel), John's version of the miraculous feeding reminds us of the Eucharist, when Jesus 'said the blessing' over the bread. Since this gospel has no account of the institution of the Eucharist at the Last Supper, it is here particularly significant. The feeding is also described as one of the 'signs' which Jesus works. The first part of the Gospel of John is often called 'the Book of Signs' because Jesus works a number of signs which show his true quality. First comes the sign at the marriage feast of Cana, where his sign of turning the water into wine is a sign of the messianic banquet. Other signs are the raising of the royal official's son, a sign of Jesus's gift of life, and the cure of the blind man in the temple, as a sign of Jesus's gift of light and revelation. Several of the signs are followed by an extended discourse, explaining the meaning of the sign, as this is followed by the discourse on the Bread of Life, explaining the significance of Jesus's gift of himself as the Bread of Life, the Wisdom of God received in the Eucharist.

Question: If you were going to have supper with Jesus, how would you prepare?

When the people saw that neither Jesus nor his disciples were there, they got into boats and crossed to Capernaum to look for Jesus. When they found him on the other side, they said to him, 'Rabbi, when did you come here?' Jesus answered:

'I tell you most solemnly,
you are not looking for me
because you have seen the signs
but because you had all the bread you wanted to eat.
Do not work for food that cannot last,
but work for food that endures to eternal life,
the kind of food the Son of Man is offering you,
for on him the Father, God himself, has set his seal.'

Then they said to him, 'What must we do if we are to do the works that God wants?' Jesus gave them this answer, 'This is working for God: you must believe in the one he has sent.' So they said, 'What sign will you give to show us that we should believe in you? What work will you do? Our fathers had manna to eat in the desert; as scripture says: He gave them bread from heaven to eat.'

Jesus answered:

'I tell you most solemnly,
it was not Moses who gave you bread from heaven,
it is my Father who gives you the bread from heaven,
the true bread;
for the bread of God is that which comes down
from heaven and gives life to the world.'

'Sir,' they said 'give us that bread always.' Jesus answered:

'I am the bread of life.
He who comes to me will never be hungry;
he who believes in me will never thirst.'

The Bread of Life

After the account of the miraculous feeding of the five
thousand, Jesus explains the significance of the event.
First he stresses that its importance lies not in the food
that goes bad, but in that of which it is a sign. They
must understand the sign-value of the food, its ultimate
fulfilment in Jesus of the manna in the desert: we do
not live by bread alone but by every word which comes
from the mouth of God. The whole explanation is built
on a contrast between Moses and Jesus, between the
food given by Moses and that given by Jesus. Jesus is the
bread of life not only as the Eucharistic bread, but first
of all as revelation. We often concentrate exclusively on
the Eucharistic meaning of this chapter. It is, however,
belief and understanding which is first explained and first
required, and only then is attention turned to eating the
Eucharistic bread. The explanation is situated with Jesus
in the synagogue at Capernaum, and – after the manner of
Jewish sermons of the time – each phrase of the scriptural
quotation from the Book of Exodus is commented on in
turn: Bread from heaven / he gave them / to eat.

Question: If this incident is a sign, of what is it a sign?

The Jews were complaining to each other about Jesus, because he had said, 'I am the bread that came down from heaven.' 'Surely this is Jesus son of Joseph' they said. 'We know his father and mother. How can he now say, "I have come down from heaven"?' Jesus said in reply, 'Stop complaining to each other.

No one can come to me
unless he is drawn by the Father who sent me,
and I will raise him up at the last day.
It is written in the prophets:
They will all be taught by God,
and to hear the teaching of the Father,
and learn from it,
is to come to me.
Not that anybody has seen the Father,
except the one who comes from God:
he has seen the Father.
I tell you most solemnly,
everybody who believes has eternal life.
I am the bread of life.
Your fathers ate the manna in the desert
and they are dead;
but this is the bread that comes down from heaven,
so that a man may eat it and not die.
I am the living bread which has come down
    from heaven.
Anyone who eats this bread will live for ever;
and the bread that I shall give
is my flesh, for the life of the world.'

Belief as Eternal Life

We always think of this Bread of Life discourse as centred on the Eucharist, but the first part of it – just like the Liturgy of the Word in the first part of the Mass – is centred on the bread of life which is the revelation of God. The ruling quotation for this kind of Jewish sermon is, as we saw last week, from Exodus, 'Bread from heaven he gave them to eat'. Then half-way through comes a quotation from the prophets, a sort of half-time booster quote. This quotation from Isaiah comes in today's reading, 'They will all be taught by God'. Its context is the personal relationship of each believer to the Lord. The Lord will sow in our hearts individually the knowledge of himself, so that each of us has a personal, secret link, to be cultivated by prayer. If we listen to the Father and learn from him, we come to Jesus, who has seen the Father. So in this reading the emphasis is on listening, seeing, believing the revelation of the Father. This is no abstract set of truths but a personal knowing, just as we know those we love on earth. Only at the end do we move on to the final topic of eating the Bread of Life.

Question: How do we hear the Word of God in the Church today?

JOHN 6:51-58

Jesus said to the crowd:

'I am the living bread which has come down
    from heaven.
Anyone who eats this bread will live for ever;
and the bread that I shall give
is my flesh, for the life of the world.'

Then the Jews started arguing with one another: 'How can
this man give us his flesh to eat?' they said. Jesus replied:

'I tell you most solemnly,
if you do not eat the flesh of the Son of Man
and drink his blood,
you will not have life in you.
Anyone who does eat my flesh and drink my blood
has eternal life,
and I shall raise him up on the last day.
For my flesh is real food
and my blood is real drink.
He who eats my flesh and drinks my blood
lives in me
and I live in him.
As I, who am sent by the living Father,
myself draw life from the Father,
so whoever eats me will draw life from me.
This the bread come down from heaven;
not like the bread our ancestors ate:
they are dead,
but anyone who eats this bread will live for ever.'

Eating the Bread of Life

This is the last of the readings from the Bread of Life discourse. It moves on from seeing Christ as the Wisdom of God, who must be accepted and believed, to the sacrament of eating the bread of life. These correspond to the two halves of the Mass, first the service of the Word, then the Eucharistic banquet. We are all so diet-conscious nowadays that it is quite obvious that the food we eat affects us. By eating Christ we are assimilated into him. But, just as, if I am sick, food does me no good and can even harm me, so if I eat Christ sacramentally without wanting to be moulded into him, it does me no good at all. That is why Paul complained that the Corinthians were answerable for the death of Christ. And drinking the blood of Christ? Blood is the sign of life – if there is no blood, there is no life – and God is the Lord of life and death. So if I receive Christ's blood I take on his life, his divine life, as the gift of God. That has alarming side-effects: it means I share Christ's life with other Christians. We all live with the same life's blood. Do I really share my life, my talents, my goods with others, knowing that I share the same bloodstream?

Question: How do you hope to grow by receiving the Eucharist?

After hearing his doctrine many of the followers of Jesus said, 'This is intolerable language. How could anyone accept it?' Jesus was aware that his followers were complaining about it and said, 'Does this upset you? What if you should see the Son of Man ascend to where he was before?

It is the spirit that gives life,
the flesh has nothing to offer.
The words I have spoken to you are spirit
and they are life.

But there are some of you who do not believe.' For Jesus knew from the outset those who did not believe, and who it was that would betray him. He went on, 'This is why I told you that no one could come to me unless the Father allows him.' After this, many of his disciples left him and stopped going with him.

Then Jesus said to the Twelve, 'What about you, do you want to go away too?' Simon Peter answered, 'Lord, who shall we go to? You have the message of eternal life, and we believe; we know that you are the Holy One of God.'

'Lord, to whom shall we go?'

This parting of the ways at the end of the Bread of Life discourse is not primarily about belief in the Eucharist. That is the starting-point, but the lesson is wider. The Gospel of John is like a series of great forks in the road, one after another leading off the true path. A series of decisions is called for, whether to follow Jesus or not. Or it is like a series of court scenes, except that people are not judged; they judge themselves by their reaction to Jesus: at the Marriage Feast at Cana, the disciples believe, then in the Temple 'the Jews' reject. Nicodemus sits on the fence. The Samaritan Woman moves from cheeky scepticism to fervent apostleship. The great scenes in Jerusalem (the man at the Pool of Bethzatha, the blind man in the Temple) ironically show the Jews rejecting Jesus in such a way that they drive others to accept him. Finally, before Pilate, 'the Jews' think they are condemning Jesus when in fact they condemn themselves by 'We have no king but Caesar'. What about the Lord as King of Israel? Day by day the challenge is aimed at ourselves too: do we believe or betray?

Question: In what does the choice for or against Jesus consist?

The Pharisees and some of the scribes who had come from Jerusalem gathered round Jesus, and they noticed that some of his disciples were eating with unclean hands, that is, without washing them. For the Pharisees, and the Jews in general, follow the tradition of the elders and never eat without washing their arms as far as the elbow; and on returning from the market place they never eat without first sprinkling themselves. There are also many other observances which have been handed down to them concerning the washing of cups and pots and bronze dishes. So these Pharisees and scribes asked him, 'Why do your disciples not respect the tradition of the elders but eat their food with unclean hands?' He answered, 'It was of you hypocrites that Isaiah so rightly prophesied in this passage of scripture:

> This people honours me only with lip-service,
> while their hearts are far from me.
> The worship they offer me is worthless,
> the doctrines they teach are only human regulations.

You put aside the commandment of God to cling to human traditions.'

He called the people to him again and said, 'Listen to me, all of you, and understand. Nothing that goes into a man from outside can make him unclean; it is the things that come out of a man that make him unclean. For it is from within, from men's hearts, that evil intentions emerge: fornication, theft, murder, adultery, avarice, malice, deceit, indecency, envy, slander, pride, folly. All these evil things come from within and make a man unclean.'

The Traditions of the Pharisees

Legal observance has its dangers, for it is sometimes easy to obey the law exactly while forgetting its purpose. It is no good driving doggedly just below the speed limit while endangering life and limb. The more exact the laws, the greater the temptation to manipulate them to evade their purpose. The Pharisees were as aware of this danger of distortion as is the modern stickler for exact observance. But the Pharisees have a bad press in the gospels because, at the time the gospels were written, hostility between Christians and Pharisaic Judaism was at its height. During Jesus's own lifetime their opposition was not so obvious. For instance, they had no share in the Passion and Crucifixion of Jesus. In any case, Jesus's own final saying here, while it may apply to the Jewish ritual Law, has much wider application than the observance of Jewish rules for clean food. It is more akin to the saying in Matthew, 'A sound tree cannot bear bad fruit, nor a rotten tree bear good fruit. By their fruits you shall know them.' A person's true qualities are seen by that person's actions; their true intentions and character, what comes from the heart, becomes visible in their words and actions.

Question: Is there any danger in Christianity of a 'dead' obedience to law?

Returning from the district of Tyre, Jesus went by way of Sidon towards the Sea of Galilee, right through the Decapolis region. And they brought him a deaf man who had an impediment in his speech; and they asked him to lay his hand on him. He took him aside in private, away from the crowd, put his fingers into the man's ears and touched his tongue with spittle. Then looking up to heaven he sighed; and he said to him, 'Ephphatha,' that is, 'Be opened.' And his ears were opened, and the ligament of his tongue was loosened and he spoke clearly. And Jesus ordered them to tell no one about it, but the more he insisted, the more widely they published it. Their admiration was unbounded. 'He has done all things well,' they said 'he makes the deaf hear and the dumb speak.'

Jesus Cures a Deaf Man

We have been prepared to see the true meaning of this incident by today's first reading, for in his wonderful cures Jesus is fulfilling the prophecy of Isaiah. Jesus's activity as he goes around 'doing all things well' is the coming of God into the world, the Day of the Lord when the tongues of the dumb will sing for joy. Jesus is the sacrament of God. In him God is active in the world, bringing peace, healing and joy. In him people met and experienced God. His gestures of putting his fingers into the man's ears and touching his tongue with spittle are affectionate ways of showing that God is physically at work in him. In a modern hygiene-conscious world such gestures might be frowned upon. But if we are truly acting as the members of Christ's body in the world we cannot hold back, and from time to time will be involved physically and totally in helping others. A famous such courageous gesture was Princess Diana's handshake with an AIDS sufferer when it was still thought that the condition was physically contagious. We too can bring Christ's healing in countless simple, but often costly and courageous, ways.

Question: Is there any connection between sin and sickness?

Jesus and his disciples left for the villages round Caesarea Philippi. On the way he put this question to his disciples, 'Who do people say I am?' And they told him. 'John the Baptist,' they said 'others Elijah; others again, one of the prophets.' 'But you,' he asked 'who do you say I am?' Peter spoke up and said to him, 'You are the Christ.' And he gave them strict orders not to tell anyone about him.

And he began to teach them that the Son of Man was destined to suffer grievously, to be rejected by the elders and the chief priests and the scribes, and to be put to death, and after three days to rise again; and he said all this quite openly. Then, taking him aside, Peter started to remonstrate with him. But, turning and seeing his disciples, he rebuked Peter and said to him, 'Get behind me, Satan! Because the way you think is not God's way but man's.'

He called the people and his disciples to him and said, 'If anyone wants to be a follower of mine, let him renounce himself and take up his cross and follow me. For anyone who wants to save his life will lose it; but anyone who loses his life for my sake, and for the sake of the gospel, will save it.'

Peter's Declaration of Faith and Jesus's Reply

This is the turning-point of Mark's Gospel. Till now the stories we have heard have all shown ever-increasing wonder and amazement at Jesus's personality, his goodness and his authority. But even his closest disciples do not seem to have seen what this implies. Then suddenly Peter comes to the realisation that Jesus is the Messiah, the Anointed of God, for whom everyone was waiting. However, Peter still does not understand what this implies. Jesus is not a conquering political hero, who will simply wipe out all opposition by overwhelming force, and make every path smooth and gentle. Jesus begins to show his disciples that the road to fulfilment is through suffering. Three times Jesus repeats this prophecy, and three times the disciples fail to grasp the lesson, first Peter, then the disciples who are arguing about precedence, then the two sons of Zebedee, who want the best places for themselves. So three times Jesus repeats that if you want to follow Jesus you must follow him to the Cross. Nor are we, later followers of Jesus, any quicker than the first disciples to learn this lesson. We greet with indignation and resistance any suffering that comes our way.

Question: Why does Jesus rebuke Peter so fiercely?

After leaving the mountain Jesus and his disciples made their way through Galilee; and he did not want anyone to know, because he was instructing his disciples; he was telling them, 'The Son of Man will be delivered into the hands of men; they will put him to death; and three days after he has been put to death he will rise again.' But they did not understand what he said and were afraid to ask him.

They came to Capernaum, and when he was in the house he asked them, 'What were you arguing about on the road?' They said nothing because they had been arguing which of them was the greatest. So he sat down, called the Twelve to him and said, 'If anyone wants to be first, he must make himself last of all and servant of all.' He then took a little child, set him in front of them put his arms round him, and said to them, 'Anyone who welcomes one of these little children in my name, welcomes me; and anyone who welcomes me welcomes not me but the one who sent me.'

The Second Prophecy of the Passion

Mark gives us three formal prophecies of the Passion, of which this is the second. He uses the triple number frequently to stress the importance and sureness of an event. So Peter denies Jesus three times, and Pilate three times asserts Jesus's innocence. Jesus is shown to be fully aware of the fate that awaits him: he goes into it with his eyes open, and accepts his Father's will, especially in the awareness that his Father will not desert him, but will vindicate him by the Resurrection.

Again the disciples fail to understand the message: while Jesus had been giving them the message of triumph only through suffering and humiliation, they had been thinking about who would be first. So Jesus sets before them a child as the model. In what way is a child a model? Children are notably and innocently selfish. Nor are they straightforward, for they can be devious and scheming from an early age. Is it that they know they cannot control a situation, and trustingly accept what they are given? The final saying suggests that it is this quality of dependence that Jesus proposes: the child is dependent on the will of the Father.

Question: Why does Jesus put forward a child as a role model for us?

John said to Jesus, 'Master, we saw a man who is not one of us casting out devils in your name; and because he was not one of us we tried to stop him.' But Jesus said, 'You must not stop him: no one who works a miracle in my name is likely to speak evil of me. Anyone who is not against us is for us.

'If anyone gives you a cup of water to drink just because you belong to Christ, then I tell you solemnly, he will most certainly not lose his reward.

'But anyone who is an obstacle to bring down one of these little ones who have faith, would be better thrown into the sea with a great millstone round his neck. And if your hand should cause you to sin, cut it off; it is better for you to enter into life crippled, than to have two hands and go to hell, into the fire that cannot be put out. And if your foot should cause you to sin, cut it off; it is better for you to enter into life lame, than to have two feet and be thrown into hell. And if your eye should cause you to sin, tear it out; it is better for you to enter into the kingdom of God with one eye, than to have two eyes and be thrown into hell where their worm does not die nor their fire go out.'

Helps and Hindrances

The Gospel gives us a rich insight into two entirely separate matters, for this part of Mark is a collection of sayings about discipleship. The first little story tells us that we must accept good wherever we can find it, not only in our own group and where we expect it to be. It is the same lesson that came in today's first reading. The Spirit of God is at work not only in Catholics, not only in Christians, not only even in explicit believers. As Vatican II teaches so strongly, the Holy Spirit is at work even in those who are seeking the Kingdom under signs and symbols. They can be better people and better Christians than those who sit back and do nothing, secure in the belief that they are members of the Church!

Secondly, the Gospel gives some dire sayings about 'scandals'. The word so translated means not stories about evil people or evil doings, but a trip stone which makes people fall over. The dire sayings are about leading other believers into evil and about the trip stones in ourselves, the disordered desires, that lead us into evil. Jesus's sayings here must be taken with the utmost seriousness, but perhaps not literally to the extent of self-mutilation.

Question: Name a really good person whom you admire who is not a Catholic or even a Christian.

Some Pharisees approached Jesus and asked, 'Is it against the law for a man to divorce his wife?' They were testing him. He answered them, 'What did Moses command you?' 'Moses allowed us' they said 'to draw up a writ of dismissal and so to divorce.' Then Jesus said to them, 'It was because you were so unteachable that he wrote this commandment for you. But from the beginning of creation God made them male and female. This is why a man must leave father and mother, and the two become one body. They are no longer two, therefore, but one body. So then, what God has united, man must not divide.' Back in the house the disciples questioned him again about this, and he said to them, 'The man who divorces his wife and marries another is guilty of adultery against her. And if a woman divorces her husband and marries another she is guilty of adultery too.'

People were bringing little children to him, for him to touch them. The disciples turned them away, but when Jesus saw this he was indignant and said to them, 'Let the little children come to me; do not stop them; for it is to such as these that the kingdom of God belongs. I tell you solemnly, anyone who does not welcome the kingdom of God like a little child will never enter it.' Then he put his arms round them, laid his hands on them and gave them his blessing.

Two Become One Flesh

The Pharisees are putting a trick question to Jesus, as is clear in Matthew's fuller account. They knew the Law, which permitted divorce, and they will quote this Law to Jesus. The Law allowed divorce for 'indecency', but teachers were divided about what this meant: did it mean adultery or a lesser fault? So their real question is what Jesus considers grounds for divorce. As so frequently in his discussions with the legal experts, Jesus goes beyond the question: God made man and woman such that they should bond together permanently and become one thinking, living being. The word used for one 'body', or one 'flesh', really means one entity, not a hunk of meat, but a single, vibrant personality. God's intention was not that they should be separable again. So Jesus does not answer the question about grounds for divorce at all. It is striking that here – and on other occasions – Jesus's authority is such that he feels able to alter the sacred Law of Moses. For the Jews the Law of Moses was God's own gift, sacred and unalterable by any human authority. By altering it, by annulling the permission for divorce under certain circumstances, Jesus is implicitly claiming divine authority.

Question: Why has divorce become so frequent? Is there anything Christians can do?

Jesus was setting out on a journey when a man ran up, knelt before him and put this question to him, 'Good master, what must I do to inherit eternal life?' Jesus said to him, 'Why do you call me good? No one is good but God alone. You know the commandments: You must not kill; You must not commit adultery, You must not steal; You must not bring false witness; You must not defraud; Honour your father and mother.' And he said to him, 'Master, I have kept all these from my earliest days.' Jesus looked steadily at him and loved him, and he said, 'There is one thing you lack. Go and sell everything you own and give the money to the poor, and you will have treasure in heaven; then come, follow me.' But his face fell at these words and he went away sad, for he was a man of great wealth.

Jesus looked round and said to his disciples, 'How hard it is for those who have riches to enter the kingdom of God!' The disciples were astounded by these words, but Jesus insisted, 'My children,' he said to them, 'how hard it is to enter the kingdom of God! It is easier for a camel to pass through the eye of a needle than for a rich man to enter the kingdom of God.' They were more astonished than ever. 'In that case' they said to one another 'who can be saved?' Jesus gazed at them. 'For men' he said 'it is impossible, but not for God: because everything is possible for God.'

(Longer form, Mark 10:17-30)

The Rich Man's Question

This exchange between Jesus and the rich man is often read with Matthew's parallel in mind, where Jesus tells the rich man to sell his possessions 'if you would be perfect'. There are no such two levels in Mark's story. The questioner has a certain age, for he has kept the commandments 'from my earliest days'. He is in the full flush of wealth, and getting rid of his riches is not a mere counsel of perfection. Jesus is stressing the danger of possessions for everyone. It is a curious fact that for many people, the more they have, the more they want. Conversely, the less people have, the more generous they are, knowing the value to other needy people of the little they have. It is not merely that we need to be free of the preoccupations and distractions of wealth. Wealth can be a good preoccupation if the worry comes from awareness of the responsibility it brings. Repeatedly, however, in the history of the Church, people such as St Anthony of the Desert and St Francis of Assisi have interpreted these words heroically and stripped themselves of all possessions to concentrate on the Kingdom of God. God's blessing is especially on the poor.

Question: Is money a blessing, a distraction, a worry or an opportunity?

James and John, the sons of Zebedee, approached Jesus. 'Master,' they said to him 'we want you to do us a favour.' He said to them, 'What is it you want me to do for you?' They said to him, 'Allow us to sit one at your right hand and the other at your left in your glory.' 'You do not know what you are asking,' Jesus said to them. 'Can you drink the cup that I must drink, or be baptised with the baptism with which I must be baptised?' They replied, 'We can.' Jesus said to them, 'The cup that I must drink you shall drink, and with the baptism with which I must be baptised you shall be baptised, but as for seats at my right hand or my left, these are not mine to grant; they belong to those to whom they have been allotted.'

When the other ten heard this they began to feel indignant with James and John, so Jesus called them to him and said to them, 'You know that among the pagans their so-called rulers lord it over them, and their great men make their authority felt. This is not to happen among you. No; anyone who wants to become great among you must be your servant, and anyone who wants to be first among you must be slave to all. For the Son of Man himself did not come to be served but to serve, and to give his life as a ransom for many.'

A Life of Service

Three times in Mark's Gospel does Jesus formally tell his disciples about his coming Passion, and each time they seem entirely deaf to it. So each time, Jesus counters their misunderstanding by repeating the need of a disciple to follow him in suffering. Today's reading begins just after the third prophecy, and – true to form – the sons of Zebedee reply with a request for the best seats at the banquet of the Kingdom! Matthew spares the two disciples by putting the request in their poor mother's mouth. Only in a second exchange with Jesus do they woodenly accept to share Jesus's 'cup' and 'baptism'. Do they really know what they are accepting, or do they just blithely agree? The indignation of the other disciples prompts Jesus to his clearest statement in words that authority in the Church is a service. His clearest statement in action is the smelly business of washing their travel-gnarled feet at his last meal with them. The lesson is difficult to assimilate, for authority corrupts even at this level. At the ordination of a priest the Church still speaks of 'the dignity of the priesthood' rather than 'the service of the priesthood'.

Question: Is ministry in the Church treated too much as a dignity rather than a service?

As Jesus left Jericho with his disciples and a large crowd, Bartimaeus (that is, the son of Timaeus), a blind beggar, was sitting at the side of the road. When he heard that it was Jesus of Nazareth, he began to shout and to say, 'Son of David, Jesus, have pity on me.' And many of them scolded him and told him to keep quiet, but he only shouted all the louder, 'Son of David, have pity on me.' Jesus stopped and said, 'Call him here.' So they called the blind man. 'Courage,' they said 'get up; he is calling you.' So throwing off his cloak, he jumped up and went to Jesus. Then Jesus spoke, 'What do you want me to do for you?' 'Rabbuni,' the blind man said to him 'Master, let me see again.' Jesus said to him, 'Go; your faith has saved you.' And immediately his sight returned and he followed him along the road.

Blind Bartimaeus

There are several remarkable things about this story. Firstly, the scene is just when Jesus is leaving Jericho. Jericho is about three hours' walk from Jerusalem, up a great, rocky canyon. When you leave Jericho you know you are just about coming to Jerusalem. It is the last village on the way, and the excitement of the great revelation of Jesus at the Passion is already upon them. The cured beggar dances on the way with them. Secondly, he is the only person in Mark to call Jesus 'Son of David', drawing attention to Jesus's messianic ancestry, ready for his messianic entry into Jerusalem. Thirdly, in Mark Jesus says 'Your faith has cured you' only twice. The first time was to the woman with a haemorrhage, who had shown her faith with great courage by daring to touch Jesus's garment in the crowd. Now Bartimaeus shows the same stubborn courage in carrying on shouting despite the attempts to silence him. So they both show with courage that they really do put their trust in Jesus and are confident that he will help. If our faith is to save us, it needs to be real, courageous and stubborn. Lukewarm, tentative faith is not enough.

Question: How do we show our faith and trust in Jesus?

One of the scribes came up to Jesus and put a question to him, 'Which is the first of all the commandments?' Jesus replied, 'This is the first: Listen, Israel, the Lord our God is the one Lord, and you must love the Lord your God with all your heart, with all your soul, with all your mind and with all your strength. The second is this: You must love your neighbour as yourself. There is no commandment greater than these.' The scribe said to him, 'Well spoken, Master; what you have said is true: that he is one and there is no other. To love him with all your heart, with all your understanding and strength, and to love your neighbour as yourself, this is far more important than any holocaust or sacrifice.' Jesus, seeing how wisely he had spoken, said, 'You are not far from the kingdom of God.' And after that no one dared to question him any more.

The Great Commandment

The basic command of Judaism, which should dominate all life, was love of God above all things. Jesus audaciously adds to this another commandment of the Old Testament, the love of neighbour. This is the only case in the gospels where a scribe positively approves Jesus. Why is this the case? The scribes were the experts in the Law and its interpretation. To stress the importance and the equality of the second commandment of love, Jesus uses a technique of interpretation common and approved in Israel. If the same words are used, you may set two passages of scripture on a level with each other. In these two commandments, and only here in the whole of the Bible, are the words used, 'And you shall love...' with a direct object. This enables Jesus to put the command on the same level – and the lawyer approves his interpretation. The first Letter of John puts it, 'No one who fails to love the brother whom he can see can love God whom he has not seen.' This was, of course, not a new commandment; it was the equality of the two commandments of love which was new in the teaching of Jesus.

Question: What sort of person do you find it most difficult to love?

In his teaching Jesus said, 'Beware of the scribes who like to walk about in long robes, to be greeted obsequiously in the market squares, to take the front seats in the synagogues and the places of honour at banquets; these are the men who swallow the property of widows, while making a show of lengthy prayers. The more severe will be the sentence they receive.'

He sat down opposite the treasury and watched the people putting money into the treasury, and many of the rich put in a great deal. A poor widow came and put in two small coins, the equivalent of a penny. Then he called his disciples and said to them, 'I tell you solemnly, this poor widow has put more in than all who have contributed to the treasury; for they have all put in money they had over, but she from the little she had has put in everything she possessed, all she had to live on.'

The Widow's Offering

We are presented with a contrast between the dignitaries of the Temple, parading in their splendour, and the least of the least. These little coins are called *lepta*, meaning 'light', hardly more than shavings of copper, hardly worth picking up. Yet the value of a gift depends not on its absolute worth, but in the love with which it is given. The value of a birthday present depends on the love which it expresses, and the care which has gone into choosing or making it. One can imagine the widow debating with herself: could she survive without these two little coins, if she made this supreme gift to the Lord. What would she have to go without? As with the Sidonian widow in today's first reading, this paltry gift is a rich expression of her trust in divine love and care, of her wanting to do something for the Lord. The little gift would go unnoticed among the riches of that exquisite and lavish building, for its splendour was the wonder of the eastern Mediterranean, but it is a heartfelt expression of her love. Just so with our prayer of praise: it does no good to God, but is for us the joyful outpouring of our love and wonder.

Question: What makes a gift really valuable?

Jesus said to his disciples: 'In those days, after the time of distress, the sun will be darkened, the moon will lose its brightness, the stars will come falling from heaven and the powers in the heavens will be shaken. And then they will see the Son of Man coming in the clouds with great power and glory; then too he will send the angels to gather his chosen from the four winds, from the ends of the world to the ends of heaven.

'Take the fig tree as a parable: as soon as its twigs grow supple and its leaves come out, you know that summer is near. So with you when you see these things happening: know that he is near, at the very gates. I tell you solemnly, before this generation has passed away all these things will have taken place. Heaven and earth will pass away, but my words will not pass away.

'But as for that day or hour, nobody knows it, neither the angels of heaven, nor the Son; no one but the Father.'

The Coming of the Son of Man

Jesus saw his mission to be the establishment of the sovereignty of God, the kingship and rule of God over the world, even in rebellious human hearts. Using the language and imagery of his time, he described this 'earth-shaking' event in terms of cosmic disturbances. The coming of God, the Day of the Lord, would constitute the end of the world as we know it. As Christians we must acknowledge that the death and resurrection of Christ utterly changed the world for ever; it was the Day of the Lord. And yet the world still continues, and we have still to prepare for the Day of the Lord, when we will come into that awesome presence. That meeting can be pictured only in terms of collapse and upheaval, our world turned upside-down. At death all our familiar realities cease, even the ticking of the clock. At death, time ceases to have meaning. We do not know, and have no need to know, when or how this will occur. For all it will come, for each it will be an individual meeting, but will it be all together or each individually? The Son of Man will gather his own, in great power and glory.

Question: Should we be afraid of death or should we look forward to it?

'Are you the king of the Jews?' Pilate asked. Jesus replied, 'Do you ask this of your own accord, or have others spoken to you about me?' Pilate answered, 'Am I a Jew? It is your own people and the chief priests who have handed you over to me: what have you done?' Jesus replied, 'Mine is not a kingdom of this world; if my kingdom were of this world, my men would have fought to prevent my being surrendered to the Jews. But my kingdom is not of this kind.' 'So you are a king then?' said Pilate. 'It is you who say it' answered Jesus. 'Yes, I am a king. I was born for this, I came into the world for this: to bear witness to the truth; and all who are on the side of truth listen to my voice.'

Judgement before Pilate

In some ways this dreadful scene is part of the climax of John's Passion narrative. Throughout the narrative John stresses the ultimate significance of the events, taking the stress off Jesus's suffering and humiliation, and laying it on his triumph. Finally Jesus will die only when he has completed his mission, and hands over his Spirit to the newly-formed Christian community of Mary and the Beloved Disciple. In this scene the Jewish authorities have denounced Jesus as claiming to be king of the Jews, not knowing how true that claim is. Jesus declares that his kingdom is no earthly kingdom, but far more powerful and meaningful. By his statement he invites Pilate to declare himself for the truth, as any judge should do. Now Pilate three times declares Jesus innocent, but at the same time makes a mockery of himself, as he stands before Truth itself and asks what is truth. Then he seats Jesus on the Judgement Seat, robed and crowned as a king. Before this Jesus, enthroned as judge and king, the Jewish authorities deny themselves and their faith by declaring, 'We have no king but Caesar.' If God is not king, Judaism has no reason to exist.

Question: Why is the Feast of Christ the King put at the end of the Christian year?

The Jerusalem Bible translation

The Jerusalem Bible was first published in 1966. It was produced by a team of distinguished English scholars (including J.R.R. Tolkien), working under Alexander Jones. It made available for English readers the findings of the French Bible de Jérusalem published a decade earlier by the famous French biblical school in Jerusalem, the first Catholic Bible edition to incorporate all the advances of modern biblical study. The Jerusalem Bible was the first translation of the whole Bible into modern English, and as such has maintained its status as authorised for use in the liturgy.

Acknowledgements

CTS gratefully acknowledges Bloomsbury for their permission to reproduce some of Fr Wansbrough's material in this publication.

Images: Page 2: Icon of St Mark on the presbytery door in St. Constantine and St. Helena church, Bruges, Belgium. © Renata Sedmakova / Shutterstock.com
Page 14: The Presentation of Christ by Melchior Broederlam. Art Collection 2 / Alamy Stock Photo
Page 38: Crucifixion by Josef Janssens, Antwerp, Belgium. © Renata Sedmakova / Shutterstock.com
Page 43: Deposition from the Cross by Josef Janssens, Antwerp, Belgium. © Renata Sedmakova / Shutterstock.com
Page 50: Christ and Doubting Thomas by Paolo Cavazzola (1486-1522). DEA / A. DAGLI ORTI
Page 76: Raising of Jairus' daughter by Johann Friedrich Overbeck (1789-1869). SuperStock